Good Friends Warm the Heart

ARTWORK AND ORIGINAL VERSE BY

Heidi satterberg

HARVEST HOUSE PUBLISHERS
Eugene, Oregon 97402

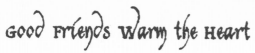

Good Friends Warm the Heart

Text Copyright © 2001 by Harvest House Publishers
Eugene, Oregon 97402

ISBN 0-7369-0735-1

Artwork designs and original verse are reproduced under license from © Arts Uniq' ®, Inc., Cookeville, TN and may not be reproduced without permission. For more information regarding art prints featured in this book, please contact:

Arts Uniq'
P.O. Box 3085
Cookeville, TN 38502
1.800.223.5020

Design and production by Garborg Design Works, Minneapolis, Minnesota

Scripture quotations are taken from the Holy Bible: New International Version®. NIV®. Copyright © 1973, 1978, 1984 by the International Bible Society. Used by permission of Zondervan Publishing House.

Harvest House Publishers has made every effort to trace the ownership of all poems and quotes. In the event of a question arising from the use of a poem or quote, we regret any error made and will be pleased to make the necessary correction in future editions of this book.

Manufactured in China.

02 03 04 05 06 07 08 09 10 / IM / 10 9 8 7 6 5 4

then winter after fall.

God gave us spring and summer,

The season that is known for snow

is my favorite one of all.

Heidi Satterberg ©

Friendship warms like a sunbeam; charms like a good story; inspires like a brave leader; binds like a golden chain; guides like a heavenly vision.

NEWELL DWIGHT HILLIS

A friend is one to whom one may pour out all the contents of one's heart, chaff and grain together, knowing that the gentlest of hands will take and sift it, keep what is worth keeping and, with the breath of kindness, blow the rest away.

ARABIAN PROVERB

A friend is one who knows us, but loves us anyway.

JEROME CUMMINGS

There is a treasure chest inside of me

Filled with thoughts of you.

In my quiet moments, I open it

And cherish again the friendship we share.

AUTHOR UNKNOWN

There can be no happiness equal to the
joy of finding a heart that understands.

VICTOR ROBINSON

When we seek
to discover the
best in others,
we somehow
bring out the
best in ourselves.

WILLIAM ARTHUR WARD

Don't walk in front of me, I may not follow.
Don't walk behind me, I may not lead.
Just walk beside me, and be my friend.

ALBERT CAMUS

A good friend remembers
what we were and sees
what we can be.

AUTHOR UNKNOWN

Can miles truly
separate us from friends?
If we want to be with
someone we love, aren't
we already there?

RICHARD BACH

A friend
may well be
reckoned the
masterpiece
of nature.

RALPH WALDO EMERSON

One loyal friend is better than ten thousand family members.

AUTHOR UNKNOWN

Friendship doubles your joys, and divides your sorrows.

AUTHOR UNKNOWN

Hold on to your friend with both hands.

AUTHOR UNKNOWN

without
friends no one
would choose to
live, though he had all other goods.

ARISTOTLE

Each friend represents a world in us, a world possibly not born until they arrive, and it is only by this meeting that a new world is born.

ANAÏS NIN

A best friend is a sister that destiny forgot to give you.

AUTHOR UNKNOWN

The most I can do for my friend is simply to be his friend. I have no wealth to bestow on him. If he knows that I am happy in loving him, he will want no other reward. Is not friendship divine in this?

HENRY DAVID THOREAU

Friendship that flows
from the heart cannot
be frozen by adversity,
as the water that flows
from the spring cannot
congeal in winter.

JAMES FENIMORE COOPER

The better part of one's
life consists of his friendships.

ABRAHAM LINCOLN

A friend is
a gift you
give yourself.

ROBERT LOUIS STEVENSON

Two are better than one, because they
have a good return for their work. If one
falls down, his friend can help him up.

THE BOOK OF ECCLESIASTES

Grief can take care of itself,
but to get the full value
of joy you must have
somebody to divide it with.

MARK TWAIN

I count myself
in nothing else
so happy
as in a soul
rememb'ring my
good friends.

WILLIAM SHAKESPEARE

A friend is one
who can touch
your heart
from across the
world or across
the room.

The making of friends, who are real friends, is
the best token we have of a man's success in life.

21

All sorts of pleasant things happened about that time; for the new friendship flourished like grass in spring. Every one liked Laurie, and he privately informed his tutor that "the Marches were regularly splendid girls." With the delightful enthusiasm of youth, they took the solitary boy into their midst, and made much of him, and he found something very charming in the innocent companionship of these simple-hearted girls.

LOUISA MAY ALCOTT
Little Women

the birth of God's own Son.

We celebrate in winter

Jesus was His special gift

to each and every one.

Heidi Satterberg ©

Watch for winter's little friends

as they gather through the day;

like birds and squirrels and bunnies, too—,

they feed and romp and play.

Heidi Satterberg©

Some people make the world special just by being in it.

AUTHOR UNKNOWN

You know that place between asleep and awake? Where you still remember dreaming? That's where I will always think of you.

JAMES MATTHEW BARRIE
Peter Pan

Savor the moments that are warm and special and giggly.

SAMMY DAVIS, JR.

Tell me what company thou keepest, and I'll tell thee what thou art.

MIGUEL DE CERVANTES

True friendship can only be made between true men. Hearts are the soul of honor. . .if a man has a sincere heart within him, and be true and noble, then we may confide in him.

CHARLES SPURGEON

"Stay" is a charming word
in a friend's vocabulary.

LOUISA MAY ALCOTT

It is not so much
our friends' help
that helps us as
the confident
knowledge that
they will help us.

EPICURUS

Life is to be
fortified by many
friendships. To
love and to be
loved is the
greatest happiness
of existence.

The kindest Friend I've ever had
Is One I cannot see,
Yet One in whom I can confide,
Who loves and blesses me.

SHULER

SYDNEY SMITH

there's color in the trees;

Against the gray of winter

like cardinals and bluejays

Heidi Satterberg ©

and little chickadees.

We need people in our lives with whom we can be as open as possible. To have real conversation with people may seem like such a simple, obvious suggestion, but it involves courage and risk.

DR. THOMAS MOORE

Friendship is born at that moment when one person says to another: "What! You too? Thought I was the only one."

C.S. LEWIS

Sir, I look upon every day to be lost, in which I do not make a new acquaintance.

SAMUEL JOHNSON

All love that has not friendship for its base, is like a mansion built upon the sand.

ELLA WHEELER WILCOX

The glory of friendship is not the outstretched hand, nor the kindly smile, nor the joy of companionship; it is the spiritual inspiration that comes to one when he discovers that someone else believes in him and is willing to trust him with his friendship.

RALPH WALDO EMERSON

A friend is someone we turn to when our spirits need a lift.

A friend is someone we treasure for our friendship is a gift.

A friend is someone who fills our lives with beauty, joy, and grace

And makes the world we live in a better and happier place.

ANONYMOUS

It is a rare and special thing to find a friend who will remain a friend forever.

RUTH LANGDON
MORGAN

True friends will say what's kind and true,

Though it may cause us pain;

They're thinking of what's good for us

And all we stand to gain.

DENNIS J. DEHAAN

True friendship is like sound health, the value of it is seldom known until it be lost.

CHARLES COLTON

I do not ask for fortunes vast
Nor seek undying fame
I do not ask when life is passed
That many know my name
But I can live my life on earth
Very happy until the end
If but a few shall know my worth
And proudly call me friend.

ANONYMOUS

34

There are many people
that we meet in our lives
but only a very few
will make a lasting impression
on our minds and hearts.
It is these people that we
will think of often
and who will always remain
important to us
as true friends.

SUSAN POLIS SCHULTZ

 Friendship is a sheltering tree.

SAMUEL COLERIDGE

A truly faithful friend is the medicine of life;

a truly faithful friend, a strong covering.

For what would not a genuine friend do?

What pleasure would he not create for us?

What profit? What safety?

Though thou were to name a thousand treasures,

there is nothing comparable to a real friend.

ARETHUSA TO ST. JOHN

Friendship is the only thing in the
world concerning the usefulness of
which all mankind are agreed.

CICERO

My friend is not perfect ~ no more am I.
And so we suit each other admirably.

ALEXANDER POPE

There are persons so
radiant, so genial, so kind,
so pleasure-bearing, that you
instinctively feel in their
presence that they do you
good, whose coming into
a room is like the bringing
of a lamp there.

HENRY WARD BEECHER

and blustery winds that blow,

I like the sound of jingle bells,

of skates on ice, and bluejay calls,

and the crunch of crusted snow.

Heidi Satterberg ©

A friend is one with whom you are
comfortable, to whom you are loyal,
through whom you are blessed,
and for whom you are grateful.

WILLIAM ARTHUR WARD

From quiet homes and first beginning,
Out to the undiscovered ends,
There's nothing worth the wear of winning,
But laughter and the love of friends.

HILAIRE BELLOC

Be slow to fall into friendships but when thou art in, continue firm and constant.

SOCRATES

I went out to find a friend
But could not find one there;
I went out to be a friend,
And friends were everywhere!

ANONYMOUS

We are, each of us angels with only one wing;
and we can only fly by embracing one another.

LUCIANO DI CRESCENZO

So wherever I am, there's always Pooh,

There's always Pooh and Me.

"What would I do?" I said to Pooh,

"If it wasn't for you," and Pooh said:

"True, It isn't much fun for One,

but Two can stick together," says Pooh, says he.

"That's how it is," says Pooh.

A.A. MILNE

Ah! How good it
feels the hand of
an old friend.

HENRY WADSWORTH
LONGFELLOW

A friend is a person with whom I may be sincere. Before him I may think aloud.

RALPH WALDO EMERSON

Friendship, like love, is but a name,
Unless to one you stint the flame.
The child, whom many fathers share,
Hath seldom known a father's care.
'Tis thus in friendships; who depend
On many, rarely find a friend.

JOHN GAY

God's blessings made it so.

It's been a fun-filled winter;

But winter's melting into spring,

and now, it's time to go!

Heidi Satterberg ©

Between him and Darcy there was a very steady friendship, in spite of great opposition of character. Bingley was endeared to Darcy by the easiness, openness, and ductility of his temper, though no disposition could offer a greater contrast to his own, and though with his own he never appeared dissatisfied. On the strength of Darcy's regard, Bingley had the firmest reliance, and of his judgment the highest opinion.

JANE AUSTEN
Pride and Prejudice

Friendship is love without his wings.

LORD BYRON

We join our hearts and hands together,
Faithful to the Lord's command;
We hold each other to God's standards—
All that truth and love demand.

DENNIS J. DEHAAN